The Intimate Relationship Journal

THE
intimate
relationship
JOURNAL

Prompts and Practices for Personal Growth and Self-Discovery

LORI ANN DAVIS, MA

ROCKRIDGE
PRESS

For general information on our other products and services or to obtain technical support, please contact our Customer Care Department within the United States at (866) 744-2665, or outside the United States at (510) 253-0500.

Rockridge Press publishes its books in a variety of electronic and print formats. Some content that appears in print may not be available in electronic books, and vice versa.

Interior and Cover Designer: Alan Carr
Art Producer: Melissa Malinowsky
Editor: Nora Spiegel
Production Editor: Matthew Burnett
Production Manager: Martin Worthington

All illustrations used under license from Shutterstock
Paperback ISBN: 978-1-63878-001-4
R0

THIS JOURNAL BELONGS TO:

_____

Contents

Introduction

I truly believe that everyone deserves to have the relationship of their dreams. And if you do, too, I can help you achieve it. As a certified relationship specialist with over 30 years' experience, empowering individuals and couples to live richer, happier lives is at the heart of what I do. In this book I'll share what I've learned not only from my education and private practice but also from my own personal experiences, balancing my career with taking care of my two youngest daughters and working on my own relationship with my husband. Whether you're looking to deepen a romantic connection or grow closer to friends or family, I am committed to helping you create and maintain loving relationships.

When two unique individuals try to blend their lives or intensify a connection of romance or friendship, success does not happen without challenges. But with some effort and guidance, you can overcome any obstacle, enhance your partnerships, and deepen the intimacy in your relationships. This journal is written for you if you're currently in a relationship but struggling to commit or if you want to improve your relationship. It will help if you've just gotten out of a relationship and you're interested in learning how to improve your relationships before starting a new one. This journal is beneficial for those who have trust issues to resolve from past relationships as well as for those who are ready to start a new relationship but haven't found the right one yet. You'll also find it helpful if you simply want to learn more about yourself and strengthen your relationship skills.

We're all involved in relationships: work relationships, family relationships, friendships, and intimate relationships. They bring us comfort, happiness, and unity. But as wonderful as relationships can be, they also bring their share of challenges. We might worry about not being good enough or being too dependent, or we might struggle with resolving differences of opinion or conflicts. It's not unusual to struggle or need extra guidance in navigating the complicated world of relationships. But the effort is worth it. As humans, we have a desire to feel connected, needed, loved, and cared for. We also long to satisfy those desires for someone else. In intimate relationships, whether a romantic partnership or a deep connection to a friend or sibling, there is a mutual sense of understanding, acceptance, and caring that develops over time.

Romantic relationships add a great deal to our lives, but most people also need other kinds of relationships, such as friendships and ties with family or "chosen family." Much of the information in this journal will provide help with a variety of close relationships, even though romantic relationships will be our focus.

Intimate relationships start with us disclosing personal information, including thoughts and feelings, that we might not feel comfortable sharing with others. Eventually our lives become intertwined, even becoming an integral part of each other's daily routine if it's a committed partnership. Whether or not we live under the same roof, we show concern for each other's well-being and take the other person's needs and desires into account when making decisions. We feel understood and appreciated in return. This is someone who we feel will stand by us no matter what happens. These aspects of the relationship continue to deepen over time as we put more effort into the relationship.

Even though most people have a desire for close intimate relationships, these connections do not just happen. They take work, commitment, and know-how, yet we receive very little guidance on how to have the great relationships that we all crave. Learning to trust, to feel safe and secure, to set appropriate boundaries, to resolve conflicts, and to weather the ups and downs in relationships takes skill and determination.

I am excited for you to delve into this journal and gain those skills. No matter what stage of a relationship you are in or if you're not in one now, the writing prompts and exercises will benefit you. You will be guided to take a closer look at where you are, with whom you want to be in a relationship, and what you would like those relationships to look like. Developing that clear vision will help you to purposefully create the relationships you desire.

In this journal you will find practical tips and exercises to help you build a strong foundation for romantic relationships. You'll learn how to successfully navigate and maintain those relationships and improve your relationships in general, romantic and otherwise. We'll start by evaluating your current relationship status and reflecting on past relationships. Then we'll shift our focus to teach you how to love yourself, negotiate trust with others, and manage conflict. Finally, we'll conclude with advice for sustaining and nourishing the healthy relationships you've worked so hard to establish. I will provide you with support and guidance along the way, using prompts and exercises that have helped my clients move from frustration to success.

My hope is that you will benefit from using this journal, but this book is not a replacement for professional coaching or counseling. If at any time you feel you need more help, do not hesitate to reach out to a professional. You can find more information, including aid if you are dealing with domestic abuse, in the resources section at the end of the book.

I encourage you to set aside enough time to be present, thoughtful, and honest with yourself as you work through the exercises and writing prompts. You might want to designate a specific day and time to work on your journal each week, creating a habit. Work at your own pace, and feel free to revisit sections from time to time. Remember that you don't have to share this with anyone. But if you feel comfortable, you can share some of your thoughts and feelings with a partner or close friend to get another perspective. Above all, be kind to yourself, and remember there are no right or wrong answers.

1

Checking In on Your Relationship Status

By starting this journal, you've taken an important first step on the path to growth and self-discovery. Well done! Let's begin by surveying the territory. When trying to create deeper relationships, it helps to assess where you are now and where you'd like to be. With whom do you want to be in a relationship, and what do you want that relationship to look like? In this section we will help you answer those questions.

"When we find someone, whose weirdness is compatible with ours, we join up with them and fall into mutually satisfying weirdness— and call it love—true love."

—ROBERT FULGHUM

To begin a journey, you have to know where you are. So let's examine your satisfaction with your current or past relationships. Consider the most intimate relationship you're currently involved in or the past relationship that had the greatest impact on you. Then list five things that you would change about or add to the relationship if you could and why.

We can have special connections with a variety of people in our lives. These connections require trust and a feeling of acceptance that can grow and deepen over time. Think about the most important people in your life. For each, ask yourself: Am I happy with the relationship the way it is? Or would I like to move toward deepening that relationship? Explore the answers on the following lines.

Whether you are single or already in a relationship, you likely have ideas about what relationships add to your life. List as many as you can think of. Describe your biggest motivation for being in a relationship.

_____

_____

_____

_____

_____

_____

_____

_____

_____

_____

_____

"Discovering an ability to love uncritically and totally has been exhilarating. It's the sort of love that calls upon the whole being, bringing all of my potential to life."

—RONNIE FRIEDLAND

What are the most important qualities of a relationship for you? Is it the love, friendship, a feeling of safety and security, or an emotional or physical connection? Think about your current life and how a partner would add to that life. Which areas of your life would be most enhanced by a relationship?

— Envision the Relationship You Desire —

When you are trying to create your ideal relationship, it can be helpful to spend time envisioning what that relationship is like as if it already exists. Close your eyes and take a few deep breaths. Envision that you are in your ideal relationship right now. How do you feel? How do you spend time with the other person? Focus on the experience of having this relationship and imagine as much detail as you like. When you're finished, journal about the experience, focusing on how it felt to be living this life. I suggest you tap into this vision daily, either first thing in the morning or before bed at night, to help you stay focused on what you wish to create. You might want to revisit this exercise from time to time and continue to journal ideas as they come to you.

What are things you are willing to compromise on, and what are your nonnegotiables in a relationship? For example, in a monogamous partnership, you might be willing to compromise about where you live but not about whether you have children. In a close friendship, you might agree not to discuss differences over religion.

_____

_____

_____

_____

_____

_____

_____

_____

_____

*I am free to be myself in a relationship
knowing I can easily get my needs met.*

What motivates you to get up in the morning—what's your life purpose? If your relationship doesn't support this, you'll end up feeling like you and your partner are not on the same page. Make a list of your most important motivations, and consider if past relationships have conflicted with them.

Core needs in a relationship are the minimum requirements necessary for happiness and fulfillment—as opposed to desires or preferences, which are nice but not essential for the success of the relationship. Examples of core needs are connection, appreciation, adventure, and intimacy. What are yours? Knowing them will help you navigate getting your needs met.

One common problem I see in relationships—even close, nonmonogamous ones—is the expectation that your partner must meet all your needs. Some needs will be met within a relationship; others can be met by friends and family. Fill in the following columns and look for an imbalance. Are you relying on one source for everything?

MY CLOSEST RELATIONSHIP PROVIDES	MY FAMILY PROVIDES	FRIENDS PROVIDE
Example: physical affection	Example: a sense of belonging	Example: a listening ear

Identify Your Emotional Needs

Going into a relationship with a clear sense of your own needs will give you a solid chance of building a mutually satisfying, lasting relationship. Take some time to think about what your emotional needs are in a relationship, reviewing the previous writing prompts if necessary. Make a list of your top five emotional needs; some examples might be affection, support, trust, patience, or appreciation. Find a quiet time when you will not be disturbed, and create a representation of those needs in the medium of your choice. For example, you might create a poster that depicts them in the form of drawings, inspirational quotes, or a collage of images cut out from magazines and newspapers. When complete, place the project where you'll see it often to inspire you to develop the relationship you want.

1. ....

2. ....

3. ....

4. ....

5. ....

In his book *The 5 Love Languages*, Gary Chapman explains that we articulate our love via different methods: words of affirmation, physical touch, spending quality time, giving gifts, and performing acts of service. Which do you prefer for others to show you their love? Is there a difference between your preferred languages for receiving versus giving love?

Ever wondered if you were really in love or simply feeling attached to someone? Love is a positive feeling toward someone. Attachment is more about getting your needs met. Try rating your current or past relationships on the attachment–love continuum.

1: The relationship is strictly about what I get out of it.

2: I enjoy their company, but I'm in it for the benefits.

3: My feelings for them and the benefits I get are equally important.

4: I enjoy the rewards, but my fondness for them matters most.

5: The relationship is strictly about my feelings for them.

RELATIONSHIP   **RATING (1–5)**

What type of person do you want to be in a relationship with? Do you prefer someone with a personality similar to yours or someone who can counterbalance your traits? Write a detailed description of the person you want to be in a relationship with.

Identify Your Values

Our values determine the choices we make in our lives and ultimately our level of happiness. They affect our relationships, our career, and our interests. Yet we often have no idea what our values are. What is important to you? What brings you pleasure? How do you choose to spend your time and money? To help you think this through, collect pictures in magazines or online that represent what's most important to you, and use the images to make a physical or digital collage. Hang your collage in a highly visible place or keep a picture on your phone as a reminder.

Considering the core values you identified in the previous exercise, which of them must be shared by your partner to have a healthy, fulfilling relationship? Some examples are respect, empathy, vulnerability, commitment, and trust.

With your core values identified, let's assess if you are making relationship choices based on these values. Consider current and past relationships, and ask:

- Are my actions and my values in alignment when I make decisions about whom to enter into a relationship with?

- Am I holding strong to my values when making decisions within relationships? Are there situations that cause me to waver?

2

Reflecting on Your Relationship History

Relationships are the perfect place to learn more about yourself and improve your capacity for intimacy. In order to create better relationships, it is helpful to look back at your past. We all have relationship patterns that we tend to repeat, even if they leave us feeling frustrated or unhappy. This section of the journal will help you identify behaviors and discover the source of these patterns.

"Love takes off the masks that we fear we cannot live without and know we cannot live within."

—JAMES BALDWIN

We all fall in love for different reasons. What is it about another person that causes that initial spark of love for you?

_____

_____

_____

_____

_____

_____

_____

_____

_____

_____

_____

_____

Think back to how you were shown love as a child. Did your caregivers express their love through words, through physical contact, through food? All or none of the above? How does this affect how you feel loved as an adult? Does this affect how you show love to a partner?

We often repeat dysfunctional relationship patterns from childhood, simply because that's what we've learned to do. Do you see patterns in your current relationships that resemble interactions you had with a parent or significant other growing up? For example, do you become defensive easily because your parents were quick to blame you for problems?

Everyone comes into relationships with unresolved issues. Past experiences can cause negative thoughts and beliefs that affect your happiness. What negative beliefs do you have about your past that could be transformed?

Example:

Old belief: My parents aren't happily married, so I won't be, either.

New belief: With new tools and skills, I can create a better relationship.

Healing Unresolved Wounds

Relationships can be challenging, even more so when we have unresolved wounds from the past. We often unconsciously recreate these situations in our lives. For example, if you had a critical parent, you might find yourself in relationships with critical partners. You can proactively begin to heal these wounds by doing this visualization:

1. Sit or lie in a quiet, comfortable space. Take slow, deep breaths. Relax any tension in your body.

2. Now picture a time when you felt emotionally wounded. See the scene and tap into the feelings you had in that moment.

3. Next, turn the scene around to provide comfort for yourself. Give your past self a hug and speak caring, supportive words. Talk to yourself as you would talk to a child or a friend offering comfort.

Psychologist John Bowlby identified four attachment styles that people fall into.

Secure: Comfortable expressing emotions, generally confident and nonreactive.

Anxious: Sees their partner as their better half; the idea of being alone causes anxiety.

Avoidant: Sees themselves as strong and independent; can seem emotionally distant.

Fearful: Tends to react in dramatic and unpredictable ways.

Which style do you most relate to? How has this affected your relationships?

*Every day is a new opportunity for me
to create the relationship I desire.*

We often repeat, without realizing it, relationship patterns in our own behavior. Do you take on a leadership role in relationships, for example? Or maybe you tend to be the caregiver. Have you noticed a pattern in your past relationships that you would prefer not to repeat?

Do you have a specific type of person you usually choose when looking for a partner? For example, do you usually choose someone who is more of an extrovert or introvert? Describe what about that personality type attracts you and how this has worked for you.

_____

_____

_____

_____

_____

_____

_____

_____

_____

_____

_____

Think back to your first love. We can unconsciously hold future partners up to the standard of that first love, trying to replicate the feeling, or look for a partner to heal the wounds from our first heartbreak. Describe what you remember about the experience and what impact it had on your subsequent relationships, romantic and otherwise.

_____

_____

_____

_____

_____

_____

_____

_____

_____

_____

_____

Identifying Limiting Beliefs

We all have fears and beliefs that can negatively impact our relationships. But you can choose to replace negative beliefs with positive affirmations. For example:

Negative: People can't be trusted. I don't want to get hurt.

Positive: There are loving, caring partners, and I am one!

Negative: What happened in the past will happen again.

Positive: With new skills I can have a different experience.

What are your limiting beliefs about love and relationships? Spend some time over a week or so jotting down your thoughts and assumptions about relationships as they occur to you. At the end of the week, review your notes and make a list. For each negative, create a positive affirmation you can say on a daily basis.

"We can never at any time absorb more love than we're ready for."

—MIGNON MCLAUGHLIN

Relationships provide fertile ground for personal growth. Choose three significant past or present relationships. For each, describe the ways in which you've grown during the course of it. What life lessons have you learned?

Romantic attraction is a particularly powerful influence on our behavior. How have you acted in the past when you fell in love? Maybe you became so attached that you neglected friendships, or you got scared of your feelings and pulled away. Consider times when you've fallen in love or wanted someone's friendship. Are there behaviors that you do not wish to repeat?

If you could improve any single thing from any past relationship experience, what would it be? Why?

_____

_____

_____

_____

_____

_____

_____

_____

_____

_____

_____

I forgive myself for any mistakes I have made in past relationships, and I move forward with confidence.

We all have a need for connection, but sometimes we can become needy, expecting our partner to fill our needs instead of being responsible for our own happiness. Do you ever find yourself depending too much on your partner, a close friend, or someone in your family for your happiness? Describe what that looks like. How else could you get those needs met?

Releasing Fear and Anxiety

Neediness or excessive clinginess in a relationship often comes from a place of fear or anxiety. Most people fall into this behavior pattern at least occasionally. I suggest you practice this breathing technique on a regular basis so that you'll be able to easily use it when you need it.

1. Pause what you're doing, and take some deep breaths.

2. Scan yourself to feel where you are holding tension.

3. Ask yourself, "What am I fearful of?" and feel the tension relax.

Identifying the core fear or anxiety with this tactic can help you feel in control because it enables you to take proactive steps to get your needs met in healthy ways.

How do you know what will make you happy in a relationship? Sometimes it helps to look at what you don't want in order to discover what you do want. Think back to a past relationship that ended. Reflect on what wasn't working and use that to give you clues. Review previous prompts if you have trouble identifying what didn't work.

Relationship Patterns

Our past can be our greatest teacher. We can learn so much from past relationships. For this exercise, make a list of all of your significant past relationships. Write down what you liked and what you didn't like about each. Do you see any patterns?

RELATIONSHIP	POSITIVES	NEGATIVES

Identifying the patterns you want to release and the ones you want to keep can help you envision the relationship you desire. Take a moment now to close your eyes and relax. See yourself in a relationship that includes the positives from the past and any additional qualities you want to include. Spend as much time and include as much detail as you want, seeing and feeling yourself in this relationship. Use this as a guide on your journey.

Relationship Requirements

One secret to a successful relationship is knowing what your requirements are—what you and the other person must have in common for you be happy. You may require the other person to be family-oriented, have good listening skills, or exercise mutual respect. Consider the following examples, and then fill in the categories with your own requirements.

REGARDING FAMILY	IMPORTANT SKILLS	REGARDING EACH OTHER	OTHER
Family comes first	Able to listen	Mutual respect	Values spirituality

3

Accepting Yourself, Loving Yourself

Now that you have a clearer picture of where you are and where you've been, let's move toward strengthening your current or prospective relationships. The first step in doing this is to love and accept yourself. When you truly love yourself, you can then show up for others in a confident and secure way, enabling you to create strong, healthy, loving relationships with them.

"The ultimate lesson all of us have to learn is unconditional love, which includes not only others but ourselves as well."

—ELISABETH KÜBLER-ROSS

"Self-talk" is the dialogue that runs through our heads all day long. Speaking positive affirmations is an easy way to add positivity to that dialogue, which helps you feel better about yourself. Make a list of positive statements you could add to your daily routine. Place these on sticky notes where you will see them often; you can also keep a list on your phone for easy access.

Practicing Mindfulness

Becoming aware of your thoughts helps you move toward more positive ones. How many of your thoughts are positive and uplifting, and how many are negative? You can gain awareness of this and become an observer of your thoughts by practicing mindfulness.

Pause for a few minutes a few times a day to check in with your thoughts, observing whatever's crossing your mind without judgment. When you notice thoughts that are negative, take a moment to imagine them as clouds gently blowing away from you. Then replace those thoughts with ones that are more positive. By doing this on a regular basis, you begin to train your mind to think more positive thoughts.

We often develop stories about ourselves that come from negative self-talk.

These narratives affect the way we view ourselves and can lead to low self-esteem. Identify some of your negative self-talk; carry your journal with you throughout the day, and jot down your negative thoughts. Then journal about how these ideas may have started.

An important component of self-love is to hold yourself to reasonable expectations. Nobody is happy all the time or at their best every day. How can you give yourself extra self-care when you're not feeling your best? Make a list of things that soothe you, and refer to it when you need some extra care.

Often we see more positives in others than we do in ourselves. Think of someone you admire, and make a list of what you see as their strengths. Now do the same for yourself. If you have trouble, reach out to people you trust for suggestions. Review this list whenever you need a reminder.

I love myself and deserve to be loved by others.

Challenging circumstances are inevitable. But in these situations there is always something to be grateful for if you look for it—maybe even something to learn or a way to grow your interpersonal skills. Choose a recent negative experience, and write about something positive that resulted. Did you learn a new skill? Did you get clarity about what is important to you in a relationship?

Think of a recent time when you found yourself short on self-compassion or critical of your own behavior or mistake. Would you forgive someone else in that same situation? How can you practice the same kindness and forgiveness for yourself? Try writing about the incident as if it had happened to another person and you were offering them support.

Acknowledging and celebrating small victories contributes to your happiness, helps keep you motivated, and builds confidence. What do you have to celebrate today, no matter how routine or trivial it may be?

Positive Affirmations

Science tells us that positive affirmations can make a difference in our lives. Psychiatrist and author Walter E. Jacobson says that affirmations can program our subconscious mind, influencing us in positive ways. And research has shown that people perform better under stress after a self-affirmation. Try it for yourself: Make a list of positive affirmations around self-love. (Feel free to use the affirmations in this book as models.) Post them on sticky notes and place them on your bathroom mirror, refrigerator, or desk. Make them the screen saver on your computer or the home screen on your phone so you'll see them numerous times a day. Twice a day, say the affirmations out loud. Do this for 30 days and then assess whether your feelings about yourself have changed.

"My true relationship is my relationship with myself—all others are simply mirrors of it. As I learn to love myself, I automatically receive the love and appreciation from others that I desire."

—SHAKTI GAWAIN

Take stock of the people in your life. Does interacting with them uplift you or bring you down? This can help you decide whom to allow into your inner circle and how much time you want to spend with them. You deserve to be around others who uplift you. Make a list of the people you spend the most time with and consider how each affects your mood.

When we seek approval from others, we set ourselves up for disappointment and miss an opportunity to explore what really makes us happy. Think about the people in your life whose approval means the most. How has focusing on your need for that approval held you back from doing things that were important to you or from trying something new?

We all have unique qualities to bring to a relationship. Learn to recognize and celebrate your intrinsic value and all you have to offer. Think about your favorite moments in past and present relationships and consider how you contributed to them. Make a list of what you bring to partnerships and friendships.

Self-doubt and insecurities can have a negative impact on your relationships. It's hard to feel comfortable when you're feeling insecure and defensive. Doubt can cause arguments, insecurities, and imbalances. Take some time to journal about times when you were oversensitive or jealous or stayed too long in an unhappy relationship because you doubted your instinct to leave.

I open myself to love, which I give and accept freely.

Know Your Worth

Take an inventory of all the qualities you can think of that make you an ideal partner. You can write a list on a separate sheet of paper or make a collage using pictures representing your best characteristics. Ask friends or family members for help if you are struggling to come up with ideas. When your inventory is complete, place it where you'll see it often as a reminder of what you have to offer.

Being rejected by someone you love not only causes feelings of sadness or loss but can also affect your self-esteem. You might assume you did something wrong, which may not be true. Review the list of qualities you made in the previous exercise. Choose one or two, and write about why they matter. When you experience rejection, review this prompt to remind yourself that you have plenty to feel good about.

When you find the love you desire within yourself, you will attract others who will join you in that love. What do you need to love and accept about yourself in order to create love outside yourself?

Self-Care Routine

It is important to practice self-care on a daily basis so it becomes a routine. Make a list of as many self-care activities you can think of: a relaxing bath, quiet time to read, cooking a favorite meal. Now take out your calendar, and add one self-care action to each day for the next two weeks. After that, consider how this benefited you, and decide if you want to keep it going.

4

Negotiating Trust

Trust is the backbone of any relationship and is necessary to feel safe and secure. Yet many people struggle with trust in their relationships. Past experiences often contribute to the fears and insecurities that inhibit trust. They can lead to avoidance behaviors, limiting the ability to form close bonds. How do you learn to trust again when your trust has been broken? These are the issues we will be taking a closer look at in this section.

"Vulnerability is the birthplace of love, belonging, joy, courage, empathy, and creativity. It is the source of hope, empathy, accountability, and authenticity."

—BRENÉ BROWN

The one person you can always count on is yourself. Self-trust prompts confidence that you can nurture yourself and deal with situations that arise in life. One way to develop self-trust is to practice speaking kindly to yourself. The next time you make a mistake, what can you tell yourself to practice self-compassion?

Trust in a relationship creates a feeling of security and confidence between you and your partner. You feel connected yet comfortable with a degree of independence, creating a strong healthy bond. Recall the relationship in which you experienced the highest levels of trust. What was that experience like? How does it compare to relationships when trust was lacking?

I only attract healthy, loving relationships.

What Makes You Special

When you are trying to increase your ability to trust others, it is helpful to rekindle your trust in yourself. The more you care about yourself, the more you believe that others care about you, too. Take out a piece of paper and list 50 things that you like about yourself. These can include your appearance, accomplishments, and characteristics. If you can't complete the list in one sitting, keep it with you and complete it over time as you observe your likable qualities. When completed, keep this list handy and refer to it often when you need a reminder of how special you are.

One way to develop trust in a relationship is to be vulnerable. Trust develops when we share things about ourselves that someone else might not like or agree with. Can you remember a time when you were hesitant to share something personal but doing so increased your bond with another person? How did you overcome your reluctance?

How do you know when someone is being truthful? One way is to examine if their words and actions match. Do they follow through with their promises? Think about your relationships. How have you known when someone was being truthful? How often do you trust these instincts, and what happens when you don't?

Relationships require us to lower our defenses, but it's common to have some level of fear around being vulnerable. You may fear being abandoned, getting hurt, or being lied to. These fears make deeper connections difficult; recognizing them is the first step in overcoming them. What fears do you have around trusting a partner? How do they prevent you from achieving intimate relationships?

Trust issues can originate in early childhood experiences, when we're dependent on our caregivers. Often our needs are not met, which can lead us to habitually wonder whom we can trust. Can you identify a time in your childhood when you didn't receive the care you wanted or needed? Journal about how that might impact your current relationships.

"Love is an attempt to penetrate another being, but it can only be realized if the surrender is mutual."

—OCTAVIO PAZ

One way to build trust in a relationship is by having open, honest conversations in which you each share your secrets and fears. Has there been a time when you had this kind of conversation with someone, and did it change how you felt about them? What conditions need to be met for you to feel comfortable sharing your private truths with another person?

Trust is a two-way street. You want to feel comfortable being vulnerable with your partner, and they need to feel the same. You can encourage trust by validating their emotions, asking follow-up questions, and conveying support. How can you use those strategies to encourage others to be open and vulnerable with you? Review the following examples, and add your own ideas.

I can validate their emotions by:

Example: Nodding and using body language to show I get what they're saying.

Follow-up questions I can ask are:

Example: "Is there more you want to tell me?"

I can convey support by:

Example: Suggesting a self-care activity.

Vulnerability Quiz

How vulnerable do you feel in your relationship? Take this quiz and learn where you feel connected and where you see opportunities for a deeper connection with your partner or someone who's close to you. Or apply it to a past relationship. Rate each statement from 1 (rarely true) to 5 (very true).

_____ My partner is emotionally available to me.

_____ I feel comfortable sharing my insecurities.

_____ No topic is off-limits between us.

_____ I feel comfortable sharing embarrassing moments.

_____ My partner is there to support me in stressful times.

_____ I feel heard and understood when we disagree.

_____ I feel loved for who I am, just the way I am.

_____ I feel comfortable crying in front of my partner.

The results give you an idea of how comfortable you are with vulnerability. They also suggest areas to work on to open up and build trust with others. This takes courage and practice, so start with small steps and build over time.

I often talk with my clients about letting go of what they can't control in a relationship. Surrender to the process, and you allow the relationship to deepen gradually. This requires letting go of preconceptions. What beliefs or ideas do you need to surrender in order to make room for the relationship to follow its course?

I easily open my heart to give and receive love.

Many people have at least a low level of fear surrounding commitment in relationships. This is understandable, given that there is always a possibility of being hurt. Have you ever been in a relationship with someone and struggled to feel safe making a commitment? How did that affect your relationship? What would you do differently?

Be Open to Receiving Love

The more open you are to receive love, the more love you will receive. This breathing exercise is a great way to increase your capacity for love using visualization.

1. To begin, sit in a comfortable position. Close your eyes. Place your hands over your heart.

2. With each intake of breath, envision yourself opening your heart, increasing your ability to receive love. As you breathe in, imagine your heart filling with more and more love. See your heart expanding as you breathe, and feel the love filling your body. Feel your capacity for love increasing.

Consider doing this breathing exercise for five minutes each day.

If you have been lied to or hurt in a relationship, it can take time to trust again. The first step is to take time for introspection. Without assigning blame, look for areas of discontent in a current or past relationship. What lessons do these experiences teach you that can help you move forward?

Have you ever been the one who broke the trust in the relationship? Reflect on what caused you to act the way you did. Were there fears, insecurities, or unmet needs? In the lines below, write an apology letter to share, or simply for your own healing.

When you've had experiences that left you feeling betrayed, it becomes easy to get caught in negative thought patterns, questioning all people and relationships. Think back to a past relationship in which you felt loved and write about that experience. Or think of a couple you know who have a positive relationship and describe what you've observed.

To regain trust after being hurt, it's helpful to focus on the future, not past mistakes. Journal about how you want your future relationship to be, with a current partner or someone you haven't yet met. What have you learned from the past that you can use to create a healthier relationship moving forward?

At the core of jealousy are feelings of low self-esteem, leading to insecurity about your partner. Finding the cause of your feelings can lead you to increased self-esteem. Think about a time when you felt jealous. What insecurities were behind your feelings? Write about where you think your insecurities first started.

Box Breathing Technique

A healthy relationship is based on honesty, respect, and trust so you feel safe being open and vulnerable. Often when people feel vulnerable, they overthink and overanalyze their decisions and the relationship. One of the best ways I have found to stop this pattern is a simple technique called box breathing, a practice that's existed in many cultures for a very long time. It is an easy way to feel more grounded and improve your focus. From this more peaceful place, you are able to develop a sense of trust. Practice this method so you can call on it as needed.

1. Breathe in through your nose while counting to four slowly.

2. Hold your breath for a count of four.

3. Slowly exhale to the count of four.

4. Hold for a count of four.

Repeat for at least 30 seconds to a minute. Box breathing is a simple but powerful tool to clear and calm your mind whenever you need to.

5

Setting and Respecting Boundaries

Intimate relationships include a degree of interdependency, yet it is still critical to establish and maintain your unique set of boundaries to prevent breaches of trust and infringements on your basic needs and values. Boundaries can be physical, sexual, intellectual, emotional, or even financial. They communicate how you would like to be treated. Boundary setting shows respect and is empowering. It requires assertiveness, but it's a skill you can learn.

"Evaluating the benefits and drawbacks of any relationship is your responsibility. You do not have to passively accept what is brought to you. You can choose."

—DEBORAH DAY

Boundaries are determined by knowing what works for you and what doesn't. Everyone has their own unique set of boundaries. To help decide on yours, think about where you want to draw the lines. What is acceptable and unacceptable for you in a relationship?

To create and enforce healthy boundaries, you need to discover what is important to you. Take note of your interactions with other people: When spending time with someone leaves you feeling drained, you need to set a boundary with them. Identify specific people and interactions that leave you feeling drained of energy.

Often we instinctively set boundaries even if we're not aware of boundary-setting as a concept. What personal boundaries have you set in current or past relationships? For example, you may have boundaries around how much together time versus alone time you need or how quickly to expect a response from a phone call or text.

Know Your Rights

If you're not used to setting boundaries, doing so might feel selfish when you start. But setting boundaries is an important part of self-care and healthy relationships. To remind yourself why boundaries are needed, it helps to create a list of your own personal rights based on your individual needs and values. Review past prompts on values if needed, and list your personal bill of rights on a separate sheet of paper, using the "I have the right to . . ." format shown in the examples. Review this list when you need extra motivation to set and enforce boundaries.

Examples:

I have the right to feel safe.

I have the right to express my needs and have them met.

I have the right to my own opinions.

Keep this list handy and refer back to it often to remind yourself of your rights, especially when you feel like you need to set or enforce a boundary.

> If you are dealing with someone who is physically dangerous or threatening to you, it may not be safe to set boundaries with them. If you are in this situation, reach out for help. Domestic Violence Support Hotline: 800-799-SAFE

Boundaries that are too loose can leave you feeling drained because they're not providing the security you need. Rigid boundaries can leave you feeling lonely because they keep you from healthy social interactions. Do you tend to have boundaries that are too loose or too rigid? How have your boundaries affected your relationships?

I am allowed to ask for what I need, and I am open to respectfully listening to what you need.

"We can be careful about our boundaries when others come close but free of boundaries in how far our love extends."

—DAVID RICHO

Mirror Work

Part of setting boundaries is learning to be assertive, able to express yourself with confidence. People are often hesitant to do this because they've adopted negative beliefs around asking for what they need. Spend time each day practicing these statements and additional ones you write yourself while in front of a mirror. Look into your eyes while saying the statements.

- My opinions matter.
- It is okay for me to ask for what I want.
- It is okay for me to say no.

Saying these in front of a mirror helps you believe them by putting focused thoughts into your mind. Looking at yourself while saying the statements is more effective than just saying them out loud.

Boundaries can revolve around different aspects of your relationship and might include physical, emotional, intellectual, financial, and sexual boundaries. Identify some of your needs in these different areas.

PHYSICAL	
EMOTIONAL	
INTELLECTUAL	
FINANCIAL	
SEXUAL	

One of the easiest ways to start communicating your boundaries to others is by saying "yes" or "no" to respect your needs and desires rather than trying to please people or avoid conflict. How often have you said "yes" when you didn't mean it? How difficult is it for you to say "no"?

_____

_____

_____

_____

_____

_____

_____

_____

It is easy for me to find the right words to express my boundaries to others. Boundaries are an important part of healthy relationships.

Saying No

Think about a situation when you wanted to say "no" to someone but didn't. With this in mind, close your eyes and take a few deep breaths. Imagine yourself in a conversation with the other person in which you're expressing what you really wanted to say. As you mentally rewrite the interaction, how does it feel in your body? What thoughts come up for you? Don't judge yourself, but just be a witness to your reaction. You might want to write down your insights. If you found this difficult, you can repeat this exercise until it feels more comfortable.

When discussing boundaries, it's important that you create a safe space by encouraging and accepting another person's views and feelings. Making eye contact, speaking calmly, and clearly stating your wants and needs establish an atmosphere of safety. Think back to past conversations of this type. Did you create a safe space, or were you demanding in your approach?

Communication Script

When you anticipate that discussing a boundary might be difficult, it helps to practice by writing down what you want to share. For this exercise, prepare for a challenging dialogue by writing a script articulating what you want to say. Remember to use "I" statements: Describe your own feelings and situation, not the other person's. And stick to the current facts only. Then clearly ask for what you want or need. Here are some examples:

"I have been feeling frustrated recently about doing most of the household chores. I need some help. Can we talk about how we might share the chores?"

"I would love to go to dinner with you, but I can't make it tonight. I had a stressful day at work and need some time alone. Can we reschedule for Friday night?"

Try speaking your script out loud. Adjust as needed.

Communicating involves listening as well as speaking. How can you tell when someone's giving you their attention? List at least five cues: They're making eye contact, they put down their phone, and so on. The next time you're in a conversation, try employing at least one of these signals. Journal about how it went.

Setting boundaries is critical, but so is respecting the boundaries of someone you're in a close relationship with. Consider the boundaries set by the person you're closest to or by someone in a past close relationship. How many can you name? What can you do to be sure you're aware of all of another person's boundaries?

Fear of others' reactions can inhibit you from being clear about what you want and need. You might fear a negative response or worry you are being too demanding and not speak up. Think about any boundaries that are important to you but you haven't stated. What fears do you have around setting them?

Physical and sexual boundaries have to do with your personal space, your time together, and your expectations around physical intimacy. Healthy physical boundaries include understanding each other's desires and limits. What physical boundaries do you have, would you like to have had in past relationships, or would like to have in your present relationship? Have you shared them? If not, why not?

Setting boundaries takes clarity, commitment, and consistency. It takes practice just like any other skill. Can you think of a time when you tried to set a boundary but either it wasn't clear or you didn't stick to it? What could you have done differently in that situation to get your needs met?

How do you think your life will be different now that you have a better understanding of what healthy boundaries are, how to communicate them, and how to enforce them?

_____

_____

_____

_____

_____

_____

_____

_____

_____

_____

_____

_____

6

Managing Conflict

Disagreements and conflict are inevitable in every relationship, romantic or otherwise. Working through disagreement is a key ingredient in the evolution of the relationship, deepening the emotional connection as you come to understand each other's point of view. In this section of your journal, we'll explore the triggers and emotions that may come up during a conflict and the positive ways that you and someone close to you can problem-solve together.

"This person is in my life for me to love to the best of my ability. Let's see what happens if I do that."

—GINA LAKE

A trigger is an event that creates an outsized emotional reaction, one stronger and longer-lasting than you would expect. Triggers can reveal where we have work to do, which can lead to healing. Recall a time when you had a strong reaction to a situation involving someone close to you. Journal about what feelings this brought up.

When you have a stronger-than-expected reaction to an event, it may be that the incident is triggering something from your past, such as feelings of being discounted, taken advantage of, controlled, or made uncomfortable or fearful. Can you remember a time when you experienced any of these feelings? How does that experience affect how you react to similar situations today?

Conflict, especially with those close to us, can bring up intense feelings like anger, hurt, or frustration. It's important to recognize and process these emotions before trying to resolve the conflict. Think about the last time you went into a discussion with heightened emotions. How did your emotional state affect your interaction? Did you do anything to calm yourself?

I listen and communicate clearly with my partner to resolve any conflicts that arise. I do my best to nurture and grow our relationship.

Self-Compassion Break

We all have times in our lives when we are triggered. These experiences can be challenging, but they also bring opportunities for personal growth. Practicing acceptance goes a long way for developing compassion toward ourselves and others. I highly recommend this mindfulness exercise by researcher, author, and teacher Kristin Neff for building compassion when you are feeling triggered.

To practice it, bring to mind a situation that causes you stress. Then follow these steps:

1. Breathe deeply, and place your hand over your heart.

2. Begin talking with love to yourself. Focus on being accepting and compassionate in your self-talk. Acknowledge and accept what you are feeling. Use positive affirmations such as:

   - I love and accept myself just as I am.

   - I will get through this.

   - I am strong and competent.

3. Repeat until you feel calm. Continue to practice this exercise so you can call on it when a trigger makes you feel stressed.

When a conflict arises, your body releases stress hormones that speed your breathing, and raise your heart rate, and cause you to lose your objectivity. What are some measures you can take to calm your body down, like taking a walk or doing some deep breathing? Make a list so you'll have tools ready when you need them.

Different people bring different styles to communication. Which best describes you when dealing with conflict?

Passive: Difficulty expressing yourself; tend to give in.

Passive-aggressive: Express feelings indirectly, such as with sarcasm.

Aggressive: Try to dominate the conversation.

Assertive: Express yourself in a way that encourages others' opinions.

Write about the style you tend to follow. How does this impact your interactions?

Communication includes verbal and nonverbal behavior. We may be more aware of verbal communication, but nonverbal aspects, including eye contact, posture, gestures, and facial expressions, can play an even bigger role. Your words might convey one message but your body language another. How can you use nonverbal communication to improve your relationships?

State of the Union Talk

Effective communication is essential for the overall health and longevity of any relationship. But many of us lead such busy lives that opportunities for sustained communication with each other are fragmented and infrequent.

To resist this tendency, schedule a designated time to talk with the person you're close with. You might do this daily or weekly, whatever feels appropriate. Pick a time and location that's relaxed and convenient for both of you. Use the meeting to check in with each other, asking how the day or week went. What were the highs and lows? One person shares at a time while the other person listens intently, using verbal and nonverbal communication to show interest and empathy.

We all have a desire to be heard and understood by those closest to us. This exercise is a simple yet effective way to spend time together and increase your emotional connection.

"Everything that irritates us about others can lead us to an understanding of ourselves."

—CARL JUNG

Arguments are a part of most relationships. But we can learn to listen to each other, respect each other's point of view, and sometimes agree to disagree. How would you feel about your relationship if you knew you could handle conflicts and could come to an agreement that would work for you both?

There are times when it's more important to compromise or allow the other person to have their way for the sake of the relationship. When both partners are willing to do this, collaborating for the best outcome becomes easier. Can you think of a conflict when you were able to see the other person's viewpoint? How did this help you come to an agreement?

Steps to Defuse an Argument

It is important to learn to manage conflict in a way that creates closeness rather than separation. Learn these rules for a fair fight, and follow them to keep arguments from damaging your relationship. If you can, share them with the other person.

Choose the right time to talk. Take time to calm down and collect your thoughts if you are upset rather than jumping into a debate.

Stay on target. Keep the discussion in the present. Don't bring up the past; stick to the topic at hand.

Try to respond rationally rather than emotionally. Use one of the breathing exercises in this book, if needed, to calm yourself.

Listen to each other. Ask questions to learn more about each other's viewpoint.

Brainstorm possible solutions. Be flexible, and put your relationship before any need you have to be right.

There are times in relationships when there's no win-win solution. To know when it is time to compromise, ask yourself, *Would a compromise benefit the relationship overall?* Think about conflicts you've had in the past. When was it in the best interest of the relationship to compromise? What would have happened if you had held out to get your way?

Sometimes compromise is best, but if that includes denying your feelings or needs, resentment can result. Giving in on issues important to you can become an unhealthy habit in the long run. Are there times when you compromised in a relationship and regretted it? What could you have done instead?

Forgiveness is crucial in any long-term relationship. To forgive doesn't mean you have to approve of what the other person did or, in cases of abusive behavior, stay in the relationship. Forgiveness means learning to feel less negativity and more positivity toward the other person. What circumstances in your closest past or recent relationship would benefit from your forgiveness?

Apology Template

No one is perfect, so we all eventually find it necessary to accept responsibility for something we've done and apologize. This isn't always easy. Here is a template you can follow that will make it easier to get started. Study it so you can put the steps into action when you need to.

1. Apologize in person whenever possible.

2. Let the other person know that you made a mistake and your priority is the relationship.

3. Say you are sorry. "I am sorry I was so late for our special dinner. I was inconsiderate and didn't appreciate all your effort."

4. Ask for forgiveness. "Will you please forgive me? Our relationship is important to me. What can I do to make it up to you?"

5. Promise to do better. "In the future, I will set a reminder on my phone so I am not late."

Think of a time when you and a partner struggled to agree on something important. Were you able to resolve the issue? If so, what skills did you use to do so? If not, what got in the way of finding resolution?

What is the biggest hurdle you've successfully overcome with a significant other or another person with whom you have a close relationship? How did you work together to overcome it? How did you grow together as a couple?

7

Maintaining Healthy Relationships

Any serious relationship is bound to have its ups and downs. Great relationships that can weather these changes are possible when you recommit to your partner on a daily basis with intentions and actions. As we conclude our journey together, we'll explore how to ride the highs and navigate the lows to not only maintain but strengthen a lasting connection. It takes some effort to maintain a healthy relationship, but the results are worth it!

"It was only a sunny smile, and little it cost in the giving, but like morning light it scattered the night and made the day worth living."

—F. SCOTT FITZGERALD

Many people believe that with the right partner, you live happily ever after. But all relationships have ups and downs. Are any of your beliefs about relationships unrealistic? Consider the following examples, and then add your own.

- If our relationship is strong, we won't argue.

- Good relationships don't require much effort.

- Love is all that's needed for a healthy relationship.

There are times when a relationship feels effortless and times when it takes more intention to make things work. What matters is to appreciate the good times to help you weather the storms. How do you handle the rough times in your most important relationships? Do you celebrate the good times or take them for granted? Give examples.

Relationships never stay the same. Changes can be internal, as you both grow, or external, like moving or having a baby. Do you see change as something positive or to be avoided? Do you go with the flow or struggle through change? Describe some big changes that affected a current or past relationship and how you dealt with them.

Sometimes one person in a relationship can change their beliefs about something. Remember, both of you don't always have to agree. Can you think of a situation when you and a partner didn't see eye to eye but were still able to respect each other? Write about how doing so can create a stronger bond.

I effortlessly give and receive love in my relationship.

In a successful relationship, we maintain reasonable expectations around what we expect from our partner and what role the relationship plays in our life. Can you think of times when your expectations caused disappointment? Have you ever felt that too much was expected of you? How do you feel about adjusting your expectations for the sake of the relationship?

When dealing with stressful situations, you want to know you can count on your partner for support. How do you feel most supported during challenging times? What actions would you like others to take in supporting you? Give examples based on circumstances you've experienced.

One of the greatest gifts you can give a partner is the gift of your undivided attention. Ask your partner or a close friend or family member if they feel you're there for them when they need you. Based on those conversations, what can you do to better show your support?

Safe Haven

Your relationship is a place to feel completely loved for who you are. To express this feeling to someone you're close to, make a list of the things you respect, admire, and appreciate about them. You can list qualities of the other person, things they do for you, or ways they contribute to the relationship . . . the way they make you laugh, how they support your hobbies, or your appreciation for them taking over household duties when you had a stressful week.

Develop a plan to let that person know why they are special to you. Share specific examples from your list. You can do this all at once or share something daily; you can share verbally, leave notes where they can find them, or text them messages. Be creative and enjoy their response. I encourage you to make this a habit.

*"Giving generously
in romantic relationships,
and in all other bonds, means
recognizing when the other person
needs our attention. Attention
is an important resource."*

—BELL HOOKS

When you function as a team in your relationship, you increase feelings of togetherness and mutual support, increasing your emotional intimacy. Teamwork requires mutual effort on the part of each individual in the relationship. What can you do to become a better team player in your relationships?

It is normal to have physical and emotional needs that we want met in a relationship. It is also important to realize that no partner can meet all of our needs. Review the values exercise in the first section. Has your thinking about those values changed? Do you have needs that are not being met? How many can you meet for yourself?

Habits of appreciation are just as easy to foster as habits of criticism. Journal about a typical day with the person closest to you, or write about a time you were together. Note each opportunity when you might have or did express appreciation to them. How can you remind yourself to say thank you and compliment them?

Gratitude Journal

Gratitude is self-sustaining: The more you practice being thankful, the more you can find to be thankful for. Expressing gratitude fosters positive feelings for both you and the person you appreciate and can improve your outlook on your relationship and life in general. Yet we all have days when we struggle to see the positives. A gratitude journal can help you change a negative mindset to a more positive one.

I suggest setting up a document on your phone or computer or using a small journal. Each day, take a few minutes to review the day's events. List five to ten unique things that you are grateful for—big or small: "I got a promotion" or "The bus was on time." If you are in a relationship, include two to five good things about your partner. On days when you struggle to feel positive, review this gratitude journal to shift your perspective.

Commitment is necessary for keeping relationships strong. It provides a sense of security that fosters love. It can be verbal, but just as important are actions, such as spending time together and making plans for the future. How have you communicated commitment to your partner? What can you do in the future? Include verbal and active examples.

Happy relationships require recommitting to your relationship every day. This can be expressed simply, such as taking time to connect emotionally and/or physically in bed each morning and evening or, with a friend or sibling, sending short, upbeat texts. What can you add to your daily routine to show love and commitment?

Maintaining closeness and mutuality is one of the secrets to creating a lasting relationship. Learning to work together and cooperate is essential, taking into consideration how an action or decision will affect not only you but the relationship. Reflect on some ways you could increase your feelings of togetherness in your relationships.

Gift of Undivided Attention

Spending time together is an investment in your relationship and something to look forward to. Here are some strategies to make sure time is on your side.

Schedule events in your calendars to reconnect with your partner or, if you are single, with a close friend or family member.

- Check in briefly on a regular basis.
- Be emotionally and physically present when you are together. Give the gift of your undivided attention.
- Ask questions about their day. Listen to any struggles they are having without giving advice.
- Ask how you can help. Be their cheerleader when they need one.

Start practicing these principles today: Take out your calendar and schedule some together time. Make notes on your phone to remind you to reach out during the day just to check in. Plan a date night. Block out time to spend together on a regular basis, and follow through.

A Final Word

Relationships, including the one you have with yourself, are a journey that provide many opportunities for personal growth. By now you've experienced how journaling is a wonderful tool for self-discovery and healing. Writing down your thoughts helps you organize them so you can pinpoint the issues that require attention. Writing can also help you problem-solve and resolve conflicts. You have taken a big step by completing this journal, and you can be proud of your efforts. This process can bring up a wide range of emotions, so be gentle with yourself and don't hesitate to reach out to a counselor or relationship coach if you would like additional support.

My hope is that this journal has provided you with opportunities to learn more about your needs, your wants, your feelings, and your relationship patterns. The more self-aware you are, the better you will be at choosing a partner or deepening your connection with a current partner. Consider going back to specific sections and prompts from time to time. You can have new insights and learn more about yourself as you change and grow. I also encourage you to use the exercises on a regular basis. They are great tools for daily life and for enhancing your relationships.

The power to create the relationship you desire lies within you! No matter where you are on your journey, my wish for you is to find support, guidance, and tools to help you along the way.

Resources

> **National Domestic Violence Hotline: 800-799-SAFE; TheHotline.org**

BOOKS

The Seven Principles for Making Marriage Work, by John Gottman. Random House, 2015.

Gottman has studied couples for years, identifying habits that can make or break a relationship. His book teaches ways of resolving conflicts and creating greater intimacy within the relationship.

Getting the Love You Want: A Guide for Couples, by Harville Hendrix and Helen LaKelly Hunt. Third edition. St. Martin's Griffin, 2019.

A practical handbook for building a solid foundation for your relationship, written by a husband and wife team of psychologists.

Conscious Dating: Finding the Love of Your Life & the Life That You Love, by David Steele. 2nd revised edition. RCN Press, 2007.

This book is for people who are seeking their life partner. It provides practical, effective strategies for navigating the complicated world of dating.

Radical Marriage: Your Relationship as Your Greatest Adventure, by David and Darlene Steele. RCN Press, 2014.

This book provides ideas and strategies for experiencing life to the fullest through your relationships.

The Power of Now: A Guide to Spiritual Enlightenment, by Eckhart Tolle. New World Library, 2004.

This book helps readers find inner peace and experience more harmonious relationships.

Calling in the One, by Katherine Thomas Woodward. Harmony/Rodale, 2021.

This book is a guide to finding love by not only wanting love, but also by learning to be available, in order to create a fulfilling relationship.

A Couple's Love Journal: 52 Weeks to Reignite Your Relationship, Deepen Communication, and Strengthen Your Bond, by Lori Ann Davis. Rockridge Press, 2019.

Love Habits: Easy Strategies for a Stronger, Happier Relationship, by Lori Ann Davis. Rockridge Press, 2020.

WEBSITES

Gottman Institute: Gottman.com
On this website you can find tools, resources, articles, and Gottman-trained therapists for couples.

LouiseHay.com
On this website you can find articles, affirmations, videos, other products, and events. Louise Hay is known for her positive thinking and affirmations.

Psychology Today: PsychologyToday.com
This website is a great resource for finding a therapist or couples counselor in your area.

References

Ackerman, Courtney E. "What is Attachment Theory? Bowlby's 4 Stages Explained." December 13, 2021. PositivePsychology.com/attachment-theory.

Baldwin, James. *The Fire Next Time*. Reissue edition. New York: Vintage, 1992.

Boniwell, Ilona, and Aneta Tunariu. *Positive Psychology: Theory, Research and Applications*. McGraw-Hill Education, 2019.

Brown, Brené. *Daring Greatly: How the Courage to Be Vulnerable Transforms the Way We Live, Love, Parent, and Lead*. New York: Penguin Publishing Group, 2015.

Chapman, Gary. *The 5 Love Languages: The Secret to Love That Lasts*. Chicago: Northfield Publishing, 2015.

Creswell, J. D., J. M. Dutcher, W. M. P. Klein, P. R. Harris, and J. M. Levine. "Self-Affirmation Improves Problem-Solving under Stress." *PLoS ONE* 8, no. 5 (2013): e62593. doi.org/10.1371/journal.pone.0062593.

Day, Deborah. *Be Happy Now! Become the Active Director of Your Life.* Bloomington, IN: Xlibris, 2010.

Fulghum, Robert. *True Love*. Harper Collins, 1998.

Friedland, Ronnie and Carol Kort. *The Mother's Book: Shared Experiences*. Houghton Mifflin, 1981.

Gawain, Shakti and Laurel King. *Living in the Light: Follow Your Inner Guidance to Create a New Life and a New World*. New World Library, 1985.

hooks, bell. *All About Love: New Visions*. William Morrow Paperbacks, 2018.

Jacobson, Walter E. "How Affirmations Can Improve Your Life and Relationships." *Huffington Post*. Last modified August 9, 2011. HuffPost.com/entry/affirmations _b_872942.

James, William. *The Principles of Psychology*. New York: Holt 1890.

Jung, Carl. *Memories, Dreams, Reflections*. New York: Pantheon, 1973.

Kübler-Ross, Elisabeth. *The Wheel of Life: A Memoir of Living and Dying*. New York: Scribner, 1998.

Lake, Gina. *Embracing the Now: Finding Peace and Happiness in What Is*. Endless Satsang Foundation, 2008.

Lively, Kathryn J. "Affirmations: The Why, What, How, and What If?" *Psychology Today*. March 12, 2014. PsychologyToday.com/us/blog/smart-relationships /201403/affirmations-the-why-what-how-and-what-if.

McLaughlin, Mignon. *The Complete Neurotic's Notebook*. Castle Books, 1981.

Paz, Octavio. *The Labyrinth of Solitude and Other Writings*. New York: Grove, 1985.

The Power Moves. Accessed November 9, 2021. ThePowerMoves.com.

Richo, David. *How to Be an Adult in Love: Letting Love in Safely and Showing It Recklessly*. Shambhala, 2014.

Rielly, Edward J. *F. Scott Fitzgerald: A Biography*. Westport, CT: Greenwood, 2005.

Self-Compassion: Dr. Kristin Neff. Accessed November 9, 2021. Self-Compassion.org.

About the Author

Lori Ann Davis, MA, has a unique and passionate approach to love and relationships and believes that everyone deserves—and can have—the relationship of their dreams. Her mission is to provide the skills you need in order to create the relationship you deserve.

Davis has a master's degree in psychology and over 30 years' experience empowering individuals and couples to live richer, happier lives. She provides relationship coaching to people throughout the world. Her practice spans the spectrum from dating and singles to working through divorce to renewing long-term marriages.

Davis is the author of *Unmasking Secrets to Unstoppable Relationships: How to Find, Keep, and Renew Love and Passion in Your Life*; *365 Ways to Ignite Her Love*; *A Couple's Love Journal*; and *Love Habits*. She is also one of the coaches in the documentary *Radical Dating*.

Visit her website at LoriAnnDavis.com.

CPSIA information can be obtained
at www.ICGtesting.com
Printed in the USA
JSHW012251020222
22514JS00009B/66